Options Trading

Definitive Beginner's Guide

© Copyright 2016- Brian StClair
- All rights reserved.

This document is geared towards providing exact and reliable information in regards to the topic and issue covered. The publication is sold with the idea that the publisher is not required to render accounting, officially permitted, or otherwise, qualified services. If advice is necessary, legal or professional, a practiced individual in the profession should be ordered.

- From a Declaration of Principles which was accepted and approved equally by a Committee of the American Bar Association and a Committee of Publishers and Associations.

In no way is it legal to reproduce, duplicate, or transmit any part of this document in either electronic means or in printed format. Recording of this publication is strictly prohibited and any storage of this document is not allowed unless with written permission from the publisher. All rights reserved.

The information provided herein is stated to be truthful and consistent, in that any liability, in terms of inattention or otherwise, by any usage or abuse of any policies, processes, or directions contained within is the solitary and utter responsibility of the recipient reader. Under no circumstances will any legal responsibility or blame be held against the publisher for any reparation, damages, or monetary loss due to the information herein, either directly or indirectly.

Respective authors own all copyrights not held by the publisher.

Table Of Contents

Introduction 4

Chapter 1: Investment Basics 6

Chapter 2: Your Introduction to Options 16

Chapter 3: Learning the Lingo 21

Chapter 4: Broker Basics 35

Chapter 5: Options Trading Strategies 43

Chapter 6: Mistakes to Avoid 54

Conclusion 57

Introduction

Stocks, bonds, and mutual funds. These are what the average person thinks about when they hear about "playing the market." While these investment vehicles are an important part of an investment portfolio, they're certainly not the only tools you can use to make money in the market. In fact, for many investors, they're just the "boring" part of their investment portfolio. Most investors who buy these investments are investing for the long haul. They're willing to put their money down, forget about it, and hope that 30 years later, they'll have enough money to retire on. If they can put enough aside, make solid investment decisions, and have some luck, they may even be able to live quite comfortably in their golden years off their investments, or so goes the thinking.

You don't see yourself as one of those people. I know that because you're reading this introduction. You're looking for something that gives you more control in your investments, more chances to improve your portfolio, more options. In this case "options" is the magic word. Believe it or not, investors don't just buy and sell investments. They also buy and sell contracts that give them the ability to buy and sell an option to buy or sell a particular investment. While this may sound strange, there's actually a good bit of sense to it too. It's actually the closest an investor can get to taking out an insurance policy on their particular investment.

You see, when you're talking about financial markets, you can often find people who are willing to assume a particular risk in order to turn a profit off of that risk. Options give both sides of an investment a chance to make money, although not necessarily at the same time. In fact, options can be either a very conservative or very risky investment options.

This book will teach you the basics of options trading. You'll get an overview of investment markets in general, a look at picking a broker or brokerage, what options are and how they're used, and a strategy for using options to make money. We'll end with a look at some common mistakes options traders make, so you'll have an idea of what to avoid.

Chapter 1:
Investment Basics

"Ignore the news. Only price pays." – Ryan Detrick, writer, www.seeitmarket.com

Let's face it. Money makes the world go round. People, businesses, and governments, use money in many ways and can find themselves with either a surplus or a deficiency in the amount of money they need for surviving and growing. Investment markets provide a way for these people, businesses, and governments, to borrow and investment money as needed.

Of course some investors are pretty cautious, while others more adventurous. Fortunately, the world of investments offers an extremely wide range of investment vehicles ranging in risk from boring old, but very safe, treasury securities and money market mutual funds, to incredibly volatile and risky investments such as futures trading where fortunes can be made and lost in a day.

Money Vehicles

Since this is a beginner's book, let's start with a look at typical investment offerings and get a sense of how they work. First, let's look at investments at the safer end of the scale, beginning with bonds and other loan type investments.

- Certificates of Deposit: you're probably familiar with these from your local bank. "CDs," as they're known offer you the ability to lock in a specific interest rate for your money. This is a useful way to park money you don't expect to need for a certain period of time, but because it's a low-risk investment, doesn't offer much in the way of rewards. When interest rates are high, and likely to go lower, CDs can be a good investment. When interest rates are low, and about to go higher, they can be a bad one, because you could be making more money off a higher rate CD.

- Government Bonds: the U.S. government often needs to borrow money. It does this by asking investors to loan it funds. It does this by issuing Treasury Bills (short term loans) and Treasury Bonds (longer term loans). U.S. Treasury instruments are considered incredibly safe. In fact as shaky as you may think United States finances are, the dollar is still considered the safest currency in the world and U.S. Treasuries the safest investment because they are backed by the U.S. government's ability to raise money and the world's faith in the country's ability to pay its bills. You can still take a risk on treasuries. Just like CDs, interest rate fluctuations can affect the value of these investments. While the government sells these bonds initially, there is a secondary market where treasury bonds and bills are sold, their price determined by current interest rates.

- Municipal Bonds: state and city governments also need to borrow money. They also do this by issuing bonds. While municipal bonds are generally considered "safe" investments, they are not considered anywhere near as safe as those issued by the U.S. Government. For one thing, there are 50 state governments (plus U.S. territories) and thousands of city and county governments. Some are more fiscally responsible than others. Unlike the federal government, which has never defaulted on a bond, there have been municipal bond defaults. There are ratings agencies that monitor the creditworthiness of bond issues, including municipal bonds. The riskier the bond, the lower the rating, and the higher the interest rate the municipality has to pay to attract investors.

- Corporate Bonds, Corporate Paper: companies often to need raise money. One way they do so is by issuing bonds and other debt vehicles. When a big company needs money for the short term, it may issue what's known as "Corporate Paper." These are short-term loan agreements for large sums of money (six figures or more) based on the company's credit rating (there are companies that rate commercial businesses creditworthiness). These arrangements are rarely longer than six months, and are frequently shorter in duration. When a big company needs to borrow for a year or more, it turns to bonds. Bonds generally run anywhere from a year to 10 years in duration, although there have been longer maturing issues in the past. Longer issue bonds tend to command higher interest rates because investors take no higher risks of interest fluctuations the longer the bonds are. Corporate bonds can be safe investments or risky ones, depending on the shape of the company. Bonds offered by low-rated companies are often referred to as "Junk" bonds, and can be very risky. They pay higher interest rates than safer bonds, but a company with a rating that low, has reached the point where the company's future is in doubt.

- Debentures: a debenture is simply another version of a corporate bond with one very important difference. While a bond is backed by particular corporate assets, a debenture is not. This makes debentures a bit riskier and so they command a higher interest rate than a comparable bond will.

Investments such as these reward the investor through the payment of interest for the use of the money. When you invest in a bond or CD, you know how much interest you will earn, how long your money will be tied up, and can be pretty sure about how safe your money is. Of course considering how low interest rates are these days, you're not going to retire off of what you make on CDs and bonds. In fact, you probably won't even keep up with inflation.

Stocks

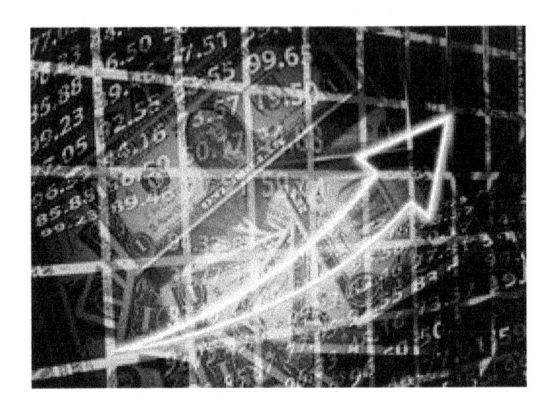

Issuing bonds aren't the only way companies raise money. For any number of reasons bonds may not be an option for a company trying to raise funds. Perhaps the business is still small enough and new enough that its credit rating isn't good enough for a bond issue. Perhaps the company would rather sell off part of the company so it can reinvest in it and grown the business without having to worry about paying the money back.

To do this, a company will create and issue "shares" in its business to sell to investors owning a piece of the company. When such a business does this for the first time, it's known as an "IPO," or "Initial Public Offering." Not all shares are created alike though. For one thing, not all shares are "voting" shares enabling their owners to vote on company issues.

Here are the types of stock companies issue:

- Preferred Stock: this class of stock acts more like a bond than a stock, even though it is sold as a share of "stock." Shares of preferred stock promise a specific dividend (payment) every designated period (usually quarterly, but sometimes more often). Preferred shares don't fluctuate in value the way normal shares of stock do. Instead, they pay a dividend, which will be enough to provide the quoted interest rate assigned to the preferred stock. One important difference between shares of preferred stock and bonds is that while bonds pay interest for a fixed period of time and then return the initial investment to the bond owner, shares of preferred stock can theoretically pay interest for much, much longer. Generally shares of preferred stock are "callable." In other words, the company can decide to end the preferred share agreement (usually not until after a specific date) and pay the shareholder the value of the stock. A company will do this when interest rates fall below the interest rate the preferred stock is paying, since the company can borrow money more cheaply by issuing new preferred stock or bonds.

- Convertible Stock: this is a type of preferred stock that once it reaches its call date, can be converted by the company into normal stock. The investor loses the interest factor, but gains the potential growth possibilities of normal stock.

- "Common" Stock: this is what most people think of when they visualize shares of stock. Common stock represents ownership of a share or shares of a company unlike preferred shares. Usually, shares of common stock also provide voting rights to the shareholder. A company can sell shares in an IPO initially. After that, it can issue new shares or authorize a stock "split" where each current share receives another share of the same stock. Because the number of shares in the company has doubled because of the split, the value of each share has been halved to balance things out. While it may not seem like there's any reason to do something like this, companies will do so in order to keep their stock in a certain price range depending on their identification of the people who buy shares in the company's stock. The market generally looks at stock splits favorably, and often there will be a rise in the stock price after a split so long as all other factors remain the same. Common stock can pay dividends, but doesn't always. Usually the older and more established a company is, the more likely it is to pay a dividend. Younger, growing companies more often plow any profits back into the company so it can continue growing rather than a dividend.

Commodities Futures

This country produces all sorts of commodities ranging from sow bellies (pork), corn, wheat, orange juice, soybeans, and more. If you or I grew a surplus in our home gardens, we might choose to sell off some of that surplus when the "crop" is ready for harvest. While you might think this is the way farmers do business, you'd be at least somewhat wrong.

You see, for one reason or another, the farmer needs to know he or she is going to be able to sell the crop at harvest, and how much it's going to sell for. One thing the farmer can do to solve this problem, is offer the "future" harvest for sale to a business or individual who wants to lock up a certain amount of that crop for a certain price. Perhaps the business wants some predictability in its costs for planning sake. Or a big cereal company might want to hedge its bets by buying crop futures every month at varying prices to smooth out its annual grain costs. It's also a way of guaranteeing the company will have enough of that product to meet its future needs.

Futures are a useful tool for both the supplier and the customer. In fact they are so useful, that the idea has gone far beyond a supplier and a customer simply writing a contract between each other. They are so useful, an entire commodities market exists simply to trade these different futures. Huge amounts of these commodities are bought and sold in the commodities markets, and while they still remain a useful management tool for the supplier and the customer, a whole subset of middlemen (middlewomen?) has developed who buy and sell these futures without ever actually taking delivery of the commodity. These people are often referred to as "speculators" rather than investors because of the risky nature of futures contracts.

The rules of most commodities exchanges allow for lots of "leverage." Leverage is an important concept in investing. The idea is that an investor/speculator can control a large amount of something while only putting up a small amount of money. Let's say the rules of the exchange permit buying a contract for 1,000 bushels of wheat at $10 a bushel. The buyer doesn't pay the full contract amount up front. Instead the buyer pays a certain percentage of the contract value (usually a small fraction). As a result, price swings are magnified. Suppose the exchange has a 15% requirement. In our wheat example earlier, that would mean a contract valuing the 1,000 bushels at $10 per bushel would have a delivery value of $10,000 (there would be some storage fees added in, but we don't need to consider that here). Based on the exchange's requirements, you could put $1,500 down to control the contract for those 1,000 bushels. Suppose the price of wheat rises from $10 a bushel to $12 a bushel. A month later, 1,000 barrels of wheat sell for $12,000. Your contract though still obligates payment of $10 a bushel. Your potential profit, if you sold your contract to another buyer, is $2,000. If you had invested $10,000 to own this wheat, you would have realized a 20% annualized return on your $10,000. But you didn't invest $10,000; you invested $1,500. Your $2,000 profit represents an annualized return of nearly 135%. Of course, the opposite can also happen. If the price of wheat declined $2 a bushel, now you're on the hook for $10,000 and your wheat is only worth $8,000. You've taken a $2,000 loss on your $1,500 investment, or earned a negative return on your money. And yes, if you wait too long, someone will deposit 1,000 bushels of wheat on your lawn and hand you a bill for the remaining amount due. In other words, playing the commodities market is not for the novice unless they're really well funded and are willing to risk losing a lot of money very quickly.

Derivatives

There's another category of investments known as "derivatives." Rather than owning a specific asset, the value of this investment is "derived" from an underlying asset and the fluctuations in its price. The mortgage meltdown in 2008 was caused by mortgage-backed derivatives, which rather than being valued on the value of a specific mortgage or property, were valued on portfolios of mortgages (often of high risk) and greatly leveraged. Once people started defaulting on their mortgages, the value of these portfolios declined to the point where the companies underwriting these derivatives (they were generally the big investors in this particular type of derivative) were in danger of failing.

There is one type of derivative investment that is worth considering for the beginning investor. In fact, it's the subject of this e-book. You'll read about them in the next chapter.

Chapter 2:
Your Introduction to Options

"In investing, what is comfortable is rarely profitable." – Robert Arnott

While it may not seem like it if you look at what derivatives did to the economy a few years ago, this type of investment was actually created to help reduce risk and give investors tools to protect their investments. Options are a good example of this.

Options are a contract between two parties. Like futures contracts, they involve one party selling the option of buying a certain item by a certain time and another party being able to buy that item by that specified time, but they don't involve commodities. Instead they deal with investment vehicles such as stocks.

Suppose you own 100 shares of stock in ABC Company, valued at $50 a share. You've owned these stocks for a year or so, having originally purchased them for $40 each. You're concerned that an upcoming announcement may cause the value of those shares to drop, so you want to take out some insurance on them to protect your gain. One thing you can do, is write a contract giving someone the option to buy those shares if the price falls to $45 a share. This way, if the price of the stock drops, you've protected some of your profit. If the stock price doesn't fall, the option expires at the date agreed upon in the contract. You're only out the cost of the contract, so you've given up a little bit of your profit, but you've had the protection of the option during the time period you were concerned about.

Another way you can use an option as an investment tool is to sell the option to buy your shares at a certain price by a certain date. Since you bought those shares at $40, and they're now at $50, you can write a contract sell those shares for $52 per share. If the price of the shares goes up past the price in the contract (known as the "strike" price), the other party can buy those shares for less than their current price. If they don't hit the strike price by the time the option contract expires you still have your shares, plus you keep the money the other party paid you for the option to buy your shares. Investors use this technique to make extra money off their shares, but at the risk of losing those shares if the price rises past a certain point. Of course if the value of the shares goes down, the other party is out the cost of the contract and you've suffered the decline of the share price, offset somewhat by the money you received for the option contract.

So far, we've looked at fairly conservative uses of options. They can, however, also be used in a way that offers the possibility of great reward, but with greater risk. It is this type of options trading this e-book focuses on.

You see, the options you learned about in the preceding paragraphs are known as "covered" options. This means that your options contract is protected by the shares of the stock (or financial instrument) you own. If, for instance, the share price goes up, and the option buyer choses to execute their option, you are required to sell them those shares (or equivalent) for the contract price. In a "covered" transaction, you already own the shares in question and simply turn them over to the buyer. In fact, many times you'll be required to commit the shares you own to the option (has to be done the same day you buy the shares and you have to inform your broker about the "joining" of the shares and option). This is referred to as a "married" option.

"Uncovered" Options

But what if you offer an option contract enabling the other party to buy shares of a particular stock at a particular price when you don't actually own the shares? Yes, you can do this. It's a riskier transaction though. Now, if the stock fails to reach the strike price, you get to keep the fee you were paid for the option and the option buyer loses their money. The danger is that the stock might rise in price and the option executed. Now you're out the difference in value between the strike price and whatever price the stock reaches when the option is executed.

Since there is no real limit as to how much an asset can rise in value, there's also no real limit in how much you can lose as well. If you sold an option to buy the stock for $42, when the stock was trading at $38, and the stock reaches the strike price, you're now out $4 a share (minus the money the buyer paid for the option). If the option were for 100 shares of stock, you'd be out $400 if you owned the stock when it was worth $38 per share, but in the case of an uncovered or "naked" option, you don't.

The Effect of Leverage

You learned about leverage in the section on commodities futures. Well, trading in uncovered options offers similar leveraging opportunities to commodities futures, minus the risk of having a thousand bushels of wheat delivered to your door. It is this leveraging ability that gives options trading its high risk and reward factor.

So while a $400 loss doesn't sound that horrible, keep two thing in mind:

- Volume: you're usually dealing with far more than 100 shares. You may be offering thousands of shares in your option contract, so now you're potential loss is in the thousands of dollars.

- Return on investment: it's a lot cheaper to write an options contract than it is to buy the underlying stocks. If you buy 100 shares of stock at $38 per share, you've spent $3,800 plus broker's commission. Your $400 loss. This is about a 10% loss. If you have done the same basic transaction through an options contract though, you probably only received about $1 per share as your premium for the contract. You would have made $100 if the contract expired without the asset reaching the strike price. Instead, in this example, you've lost $400, or four times the amount you stood to gain. The more value the asset gains before the contract is executed by the buyer, the greater your loss. The more shares of the asset covered by the contract, the greater your loss too.

The explanation above is over simplified a bit since this is a beginner e-book. You'll learn more about options in greater detail in the upcoming chapters. The next chapter introduces you to the language of options trading.

Chapter 3:
Learning the Lingo

"How many millionaires do you know who have become wealthy by investing in savings accounts? I rest my case." – Robert G. Allen

There are a lot of terms and language a novice options trader needs to learn before beginning to invest. You'll learn about them in this chapter, as well as gaining more insight into what they are about.

Let's start with the basic vocabulary. We've already covered "options," "leverage," "strike price," and "covered." There's still a lot more to go.

Basic Terms

- Writer: this is the individual offering the options contract.

- Volatility: refers to the frequency and degree of movement an asset's price can take. Some assets offer high volatility (frequent and large price swings), some don't. Low volatility assets tend to be considered more appropriate for conservative portfolios, while high volatility assets tend to be more appropriate for aggressive portfolios.

- Hedging: a method used to reduce investment risk. Using "married" or "covered" (not the same thing), options where the writer owns the assets the options are written for, can protect the asset owner from volatility.

- Beta: this is a measure of an asset's volatility compared to that of other securities in the same market.

We also have language for the actual options themselves. These terms describe whether the option is for buying or selling the asset and the prices involved. The challenge is that traders often use a variety of synonyms for these basic terms.

- Calls (Call options): the option writer uses these to give the buyer the ability to buy an asset when it reaches a specific price.

- Puts (Put options): the option writer uses these to give the buyer the ability to sell an asset when it reaches a specified price.

- Expiration: options contracts are written for a specific period of time. This can range from a few days, all the way to a few years or longer. As you might expect, the longer the contract, the higher the price the option buyer will pay.

- Premium: this is the price the buyer pays for the options.

- Employee Stock Option: Higher-ranking company employees often receive stock options as part of their compensation. These options grant the recipient the right to buy a specific number of shares at a fixed price. If the company's stock value goes up, the employee can exercise the stock option to benefit from the increase. If the company stock fails to rise in value, the employee doesn't make any money off the option. The idea is that the options are only worth something if the company's value is increased, motivating the employees to do their best.

- Contract size: generally 100 shares when buying or selling an option on a particular stock. The price of the option will be given per share. Example: a $2 option for 100 shares would cost $200.

Options traders also have terms they use to describe where the option is in its life. These terms refer to the "moneyness" of the option.

- In the money: the asset has achieved the required price movement to reward the buyer

- Out of the money: the asset has not achieved the price necessary to reward the option buyer

- At the money: the asset is at the price necessary to activate the option terms for the buyer.

Investors also have terms to specify their market approach and evaluation. These terms indicate whether a trader is optimistic or pessimistic about the particular market.

- Bulls, bullish: plays off the idea that bulls are aggressive animals that charge forward. A "bullish" trader is optimistic that the market prices are going to rise or continue to rise.

- Bears, bearish: plays on the idea of bears being lumbering animals that hibernate for long stretches of time. A "bearish" trader is pessimistic about the market's prospects. He or she may sit on the sidelines (not invest at all) or make investments to take advantage of the market downturn they anticipate.

- Going long: the trader is bullish on the market or a particular asset.

- Going short: the trader is bearish on the market or a particular asset. Not the same as "selling short," which will be explained in the paragraph on buying/selling language.

- Contrarian investor: some investors feel the best approach is to defy the prevailing opinion and invest in the opposite direction of everyone else.

Sometimes only part of an investment market will be rising while the rest of that market may be declining, or falling when the rest of the market is rising. Since markets are made up of large numbers of companies/assets, it shouldn't be surprising that different parts are moving in different directions. One thing to remember is that you can make money no matter which direction the market is moving in.

There are a variety of terms traders use to describe their maneuvers. Let's look at them next in the paragraph on buying/selling language:

- Bid: the price a potential buyer is willing to pay for an asset

- Ask: the price a potential seller is willing to sell the asset for

- Bid/ask spread: this refers to the difference between the bid and ask prices.

- Selling short: this is a bearish technique investors use when they expect the price of an asset to decline. The investor "borrows" the asset, usually from a broker, and then sells it at the current market price. If the asset price declines, the investor can then replace the borrowed asset with one that cost less than what the investor sold the original asset for. Of course, asset prices can rise as well as fall. If the asset in question goes up in price rather than down, the short seller must still replace the borrowed asset, but now must pay more for the replacement, thus losing money. Short sales can be quite risky because the best the short seller can do is double their money if the asset value declines to nothing, but an asset's price can increase with no limit.

- Uptick rule: short sales have been controversial at times. Often, investors blame short sales for market declines, even though every short sale guarantees future stock purchases (to replace the shorted shares). Uptick rules (if they exist for the asset you're following) prevent short sellers from shorting an asset unless its price has "ticked" upward.

Margin

So you've learned about leverage and its power. Buying assets "on margin" is one way of utilizing leverage. Let's say you want to buy shares of a stock. You can either pay the full price per share plus commission, or you can borrow money from your broker, putting up some of your money too. In this way, you can multiply the power of your money. Let's say your broker will let you buy on a 50% margin. This means you're putting up $1 of your money for every $2 of stock you buy (plus the interest your broker charges for using its money). Since you can buy twice as much stock this way, your potential profits – and potential losses – can double.

There are some issues with buying on margin though; depending on the market you're investing in. For stocks, the SEC (Securities and Exchange Commission) determines what margin amount brokers are allowed to offer (they can offer tighter margin requirements, but can't exceed the SEC maximum). If your investment value drops below a certain amount (known as the "maintenance margin"), your broker will either require you to put up more money, or, will sell enough of your investment to bring your position back up to the required margin percentage. Your broker isn't required to tell you they are selling off your stock either.

Margin accounts are usually required to maintain a minimum of a $25,000 to $30,000. If the balance falls below that amount, your broker will once again require you to bring it up to the required minimum. Your margin account must be held as a separate trading account. You can't co-mingle funds for other purposes.

Brokers, Brokerages, and Floor Brokers

Once you're ready to start trading, you're going to need to find someone to handle your transactions for you. This person or company is known as a broker, and there are several different types.

A "broker" is someone who acts as the middleman (woman) who handles buying and selling assets between investors. Brokers fall into two categories: full commission brokers and discount brokers. Here's a breakdown of each:

- Full Commission Broker: this is the traditional broker. They provide advice, handle paperwork, manage accounts (even buying and selling at their discretion depending on the broker/client relationship), and charge the "full" commission rate, which will vary depending on the size of your account.

- Discount Broker: these brokers discount their services and count on large numbers of clients to succeed. A discount broker won't offer specific advice (they may publish a newsletter or investment guide sent to all their clients), handle paperwork, or manage your account for you. This is fine for many of today's investors, who want to take charge of their investments rather than rely on a broker. Options traders usually prefer discount brokers to help keep their costs down. Traders do need to do their research before selecting a broker (something the next chapter covers) since extra fees can eat into your resources.

- Brokerage: a "brokerage," of "brokerage house," is simply a collection of brokers who are part of a company designed for investment management.

Option Types

There are two basic approaches to how options are created and managed. These are known as "American Style Options," and "European Style Options." While there are similarities between the two types, it's what they do differently that's important here.

While you may think that they use European style in Europe and American style in the United States, that isn't the case. Instead, it varies from investment option to investment option.

Perhaps the most significant difference between the two is that holders of American style can execute their option at any time before the expiration date. Holders of European style option do not. Obviously, this can be a big deal depending on the volatility of the investment.

Another difference is the two option styles expire on different days of the week. American style typically expires on the third Friday of the month the contract ends. European style options expire the third Thursday of the month the contract ends.

Generally, stocks and ETFs (Exchange Traded Funds, a type of open ended fund that can be traded just like stocks) trade under the American style. With stock indices, most trade under the European option style (limited indices such as the S&P 100 are an exception).

Binary Options

These are a special type of option with only a put or call choice. They are very simple propositions of the "yes/no" variety. An example would be a binary option for the price of a stock being greater than $100 share by 4 p.m. You will have a choice of a bid or ask price, which are set by traders based on the perceived likelihood of one being more likely to win.

Binary options bid/ask prices will always be between $100 and $0. If traders feel the likelihood of one side or the other is close, you'll likely see a bid/ask of around $49/$51. If there's a great likelihood of the stock exceeding the target price by the deadline, then the bid/ask might be closer to $85/$87 or higher.

Let's say you paid $51 for your binary option and the stock makes good. You'll receive the $100 value of the binary option. This gives you a profit of $49 minus commission or fees. You are "in the money." If the stock fails to beat the target price, then you're out the $51 plus commission or fees. You are "out of the money."

The bid and ask price will fluctuate depending on the stock price's movement before the deadline. Because they are so simple, binary options are popular choices for beginning investors and those without a lot of time to spend managing their money. You can purchase more than one binary option contract increasing your profit or loss potential.

Settlement Price Determination

Another difference between the two option styles is how and when the option settlement price is determined. The settlement price for American style options is determined by the regular closing price of the asset at the end of the trading day the third Friday of the month. Trades that occur after hours do not have any effect on this price. With European style options, the settlement price usually isn't known until sometime during the next trading day.

Other Terms

- "Automatic" Exercise: your broker will exercise the expiring option to protect you.

- Auto Trading: you can make an agreement with your broker to automatically execute a position if certain market conditions are met.

- Open/Close: beginning and ending of the trading day. Also used to refer to a security's price at either point. For example: "Shares of ABC Corporation opened higher this morning (or closed lower this afternoon)."

- Correction: a stock price drop that quickly rebounds

- Decay/Time Decay: refers to the gradual reduction in time left for the option contract.

- Dividend: companies reward stockholders one of two ways. The price of the stock can increase or the company can share profits with shareholders by paying them some of those profits per shares held by each stockholder. These payments are called dividends. Generally the price of the stock declines by an amount similar to the dividend, since the company is worth less after paying out that money. If you hold an option for a stock that pays out a dividend during the contract period, the value of that dividend has to be factored into the stock price.

- Fundamentals: some investors base their investment decisions on readily available information on a company's finances, assets, and other historical data. These include share price versus historical share price, price to earnings ratio [P/E], cash flow, return on assets, etc.

- Technical Analysis: these investors rely on analyzing the behavior of a stock or stocks and looks for indicators they feel predict movement.

Indexes and Index Options

How is the "market" doing? Wouldn't it be nice if there were a simple to track the overall stock market or bond market or any other market? Well, there is actually. You've probably even heard of some of them, such as the Dow Jones Industrial Average, Standard & Poor's 500, NASDAQ, etc. These are indexes of selected stocks whose value is represented by a number. You can follow these indexes and keep track of their change in value on a percentage basis to see how well or how poorly the market is doing. These index numbers don't necessarily mean that a stock you hold is doing as well or as poorly as its market index might indicate, but they do give a broad impression of how a particular market is performing.

Suppose you aren't interested in following and investing in a single stock or bond? Instead, you'd rather invest in an index, since this would provide you with greater diversity. There are several ways you can do this. One way is by investing in a mutual fund that tracks a particular index. It does this by buying shares in the companies of a particular index and then creating a fund investors can buy shares of so they can match (closely but not necessarily exactly), the performance of that particular index. Vanguard's Index 500 Fund is a very popular mutual fund that mirrors the performance of the S&P 500.

Besides providing its investors with the diversity of the 500 stocks of that index, the fund also keeps its expenses very low since there aren't big management fees or other costs normally incurred by actively managed funds.

Another way to use indexes for your investment strategy is through buying Index Options. Now, instead of buying shares in a mutual fund, you're buying options whose value tracks the performance of the particular index. Unlike a stock option, which is based on the performance of the underlying stock, index options have no underlying asset except the performance of the index itself. There is no investment in the actual stocks or bonds that make up the index. If this sounds a little like gambling, you're not that far off. Index options are simply cash instruments. There is no buying or selling of stock involved. Still, if you're more confident in your ability to predict how a particular index will do compared to an individual stock, then index options could be the way to go. Unlike stocks, bonds, and mutual funds, whose values fluctuate throughout the day, index prices are only calculated at the end of the trading day.

Now that you've learned about the main vocabulary of options trading (yes, there is more, but we've covered the main stuff), it's time to learn about choosing a broker and what they can do for you.

Chapter 4: Broker Basics

"Every one in a while, the market does something so stupid, it takes your breath away." – Jim Cramer

Choosing the right broker can make your trading life easier, save you money on expenses, and help you manage your trades efficiently. There's been a lot of debate regarding the value of traditional brokers versus discount brokers, but for an options trader, the choice is fairly simple, your best bet may be a discount broker.

If you're considering options trading because you want to take control of your investments and take advantage of the opportunities that options offer, then a discount broker is probably the best way to go. If you're a novice in the options trading world and want professional help, then perhaps a full service broker is a better choice.

As you learned in the previous chapter, there's a fair bit of difference between the two types of brokers. Over the years each has added some of the other's features, to further entice traders to chose them, but so, they still serve different purposes.

Let's look at each from the perspective of someone who wants to get into options trading. We'll start with the traditional broker.

Full Service (traditional) Brokers

Discount brokers are a relatively new phenomenon in the investment world. Their popularity has caused many traditional brokers to make changes to their approach. It's now possible to find a full service broker who lets you pick and choose many of the services they provide to you, rather than simply managing your account.

They can be a good choice for investors who are unsure of their abilities or are new to the market. They are also popular with investors who don't have the time to properly search for and research good investment opportunities.

The downside is using a traditional broker is going to cost more than using a discount broker. Another potential problem for small investors is that a full-service broker may have minimum account requirements beyond what the small investor can afford. An additional risk is that since these brokers are generally paid by the trade rather than by how well your account does, they can have an incentive to trade more frequently to improve their commissions. This can lead to "churning" where trades are made frequently. Thankfully, most reputable brokers don't do this. The possibility of it though, is one more reason to thoroughly research a traditional broker before hiring one.

You've likely heard of many established full-service brokers. Dean Witter, Smith Barney, Morgan Stanley, Merrill Lynch, and others belong in this group. There are also many individual and small brokerage operations to choose from. Let's consider some benefits/drawbacks of traditional brokers:

Benefits of Using a Traditional Broker

The traditional broker can make your trading life easier and less complicated. It can also open up more opportunities for you than trading via a discount broker. Here are some other benefits:

- Research: full service brokerage houses will have their own research analysts. These analysts have a lot of experience and education in searching for and evaluating investment opportunities.

- Guidance: experienced brokers can help you determine your investment comfort level, identify markets and investments that match your needs, and help you avoid making fundamental mistakes.

- Opportunities: full service brokers can frequently offer you access to investments you wouldn't normally have access to investing on your own.

- Administrative: a full service broker can make your life a bit easier by taking care of a lot of the administrative concerns involved in managing your investments.

- Customized service: a full service broker can help you determine the proper asset allocation (proper diversification) to meet your needs. This can extend to things like estate planning.

- Personal care: if you're more comfortable dealing with a human being rather than a web site, having a broker you can call or meet with can make you feel more comfortable. After all, you're trusting them with your money. It's not unreasonable to want to work with someone you're confident in.

Disadvantages of Using a Traditional Broker

There are of course, disadvantages to going with a traditional broker. These include:

- Fees: traditional brokers charge more for executing transactions and usually have more fees to other services.

- Account minimums: every broker is going to have a minimum account requirement. Traditional brokers generally call for higher minimums than discount brokers, although they have become more competitive. A few, are even offering flat trading rates for investors who prefer to function primarily on their own.

- Withdrawals: it's not necessarily harder to pull money from an account with a traditional broker than it is a discount broker, but it is important to make sure the one you're considering doesn't place any hurdles or fees in your way if you do want to withdrawal your money. Some brokers give you the ability to write checks against your account (additional fees may apply).

- Churn: just because most reputable full service brokers try to avoid "churning" their client's accounts, doesn't guarantee that every broker will.

Advantages of Using a Discount Broker

The less you feel you need help, the more sense a discount broker makes for you. The lower transaction costs and other fees can make it worthwhile for you to use one. The ranks of discount brokers include: Charles Schwab, TD Ameritrade, OptionsHouse, Scottrade, and others. Here are some of the advantages of discount brokers:

- Lower prices: this the strength of discount brokers, so if managing trading expenses is a high priority for you, they're the way to go.

- The investor is in control: you have no worries about your broker churning you account to make more in commissions. You also don't have to worry about a broker pushing a stock on you that you're not interested in.

- Trading platforms: many discount brokers offer their own trading software geared towards the self-trader, making it easier for you to manage your investments.

- Smaller account minimums: discount brokers generally require smaller account minimums except where required by regulations. You'll probably be able to open a trading account with less money, but a margin account will still have to have the minimum amount required by the SEC.

Of course choosing a discount broker does mean giving up some of the benefits you get from a traditional broker. Whether or not these benefits out weigh the gains is up to the individual trader to decide. As the line between traditional brokers and discount traders blurs (as each tries to make itself more attractive to a greater variety of investors) it becomes easier for you to find a broker that meets your needs at the best cost. Still, discount brokers do have some disadvantages.

- You're pretty much on your own: discount brokers don't offer much in the way of services or hand holding, in part because those things drive up expenses. You also won't have a consistent individual to meet with in person, or perhaps even online.

- Fewer offerings: discount brokers seldom offer as many investment options as full service brokers do.

- Fewer benefits to infrequent traders: since the big advantage of discount brokers is that you'll spend less to make trades, the fewer trades you make, the less you benefit. If you're an occasional trader, finding a full service broker who understands your needs and goals may be a better choice.

So how do you find the right broker? First you need to figure out who you are as an investor? How comfortable are you with risk? How independent are you? How confident are you in your ability to pick and manage investments? How well educated are you when it comes to investment management?

How much money do you have to invest? How much money can you afford to lose? What kind of investments are you interested in? What market sectors are you interested in or knowledgeable about?

If you're interested in trading options, then looking for a broker who focuses on this area is a good idea. Here are some other things you should consider before choosing a broker.

- Customer service: how's the broker's reputation for taking care of its customers. How hard is it to talk to someone at the brokerage. Does it offer live help online?

- Product selection: does it handle the type of investments you are interested in trading?

- Trading alternatives: what happens if you can't get online? Does the broker offer an alternative such as phoning in an order?

- Broker's background and reputation: what is the broker's origin? How do its customers view it? You can find online reviews for brokers at various web sites. Some are "professional" reviews by knowledgeable investment writers; others are personal reviews by traders who've used the brokerage. Both types are valuable in helping you judge a broker.

- How do they treat the cash in your account: it's rare for an investor to not have some cash in a trading account. Does the broker pay interest on that money? It should.

- Speed and quality of executions: delays or mistakes in executing your investment orders can cost you money.

What this broker's reputation for handling transactions?

- Security of your account: how's the broker's record on security? Does it have any history of accounts being hacked or disrupted?

Picking a broker is an important task for a beginning trader. The right broker can be an asset in your trading efforts. The wrong one can cost you money and opportunities. Once you picked a broker, monitor them. Re-evaluate them from time to time. If you're not satisfied with its performance, maybe you should start looking for a new broker. This is a business relationship, not a marriage.

Choose wisely.

Chapter 5:
Options Trading Strategies

"I will tell you how to become rich. Close the doors. Be fearful when others are greedy. Be greedy when others are fearful."
– Warren Buffet

It's time to start planning your trading career. There are some important things to do right from the start. The first is to keep a trading journal that records your successes and failures and what you've learned from them.

A second record should be a listing of transactions. Include the asset, start price, target end price, commission and fees paid, and target date. You should have a trading plan for every trade you execute. Make sure your plan includes things like exit parameters (what profit or loss will cause you to exit the position). Also note any possible events that could affect the underlying asset price (such as a shareholder report coming out during the period you're holding the option) and how it might affect the option price.

Since you're a smart trader, you're also going to maintain a list of potential stocks or investment vehicles you're considering. Each potential investment should be properly researched and considered. You can then make a decision as to which of these possible investments is the best one for you and what trading strategy seems to be indicated by your rescarch.

One other thing you should do is determine when you are going to get out of the investment. Remember, there are two things you must do in a stock transaction: buy a stock and sell that stock. To make a profit, you have to manage to sell the stock for more than you paid for with enough of a profit to cover commissions and fees and give you a decent return. Traders use a variety of approaches to figure out when they should exit a position. These include:

- Change in fundamental or technical analysis: the trader has analyzed a stock and found it to meet his or her criteria for a growth investment. At some point the stock reaches a point where it is priced to a point where its fundamental analysis or technical analysis (whichever approach they're using) indicates it's over priced.

- Targeted return: some traders will determine a price at which they will automatically exit their position. In fact they may pick both a high and a low price for such decision and issue orders to their broker to sell the stock at those points.

- Time based exit: an investor's stock analysis may include a deadline for exiting the position. Perhaps they feel a change of seasons will affect the stock price, or a retailer may peak at the end of a shopping period. Whatever the reason, the trader can instruct his or her broker to automatically sell the asset on a particular date.

Also make sure you have a quiet, useable work area and a reliable Internet connection. Also be sure to have a backup method of getting online or reaching your broker if your Internet connection or phone service goes down.

There are a number of trading strategies available to options traders. There are also some interesting assets for options traders choose from. Let's start with some simple ones.

First off, there are the conservative approaches. If you're reluctant to take on risk, then trading in covered or married options will subject you to less risk, but also less reward. Trading "naked" options (options not backed by the appropriate stocks) will do the opposite. Keep in mind, brokers may limit or prohibit you from trading naked options as a beginner, so you may have to start with covered trades.

Index Options

This type of option is simple, relatively inexpensive, and not that risky. Index Options can be a good choice for beginning traders because you don't need a big dollar trading account or years of experience to be able to trade them. (Many brokers for instance won't let beginning traders trade naked options.) While investing in these options isn't exactly a "strategy" it is a good option for novice options traders, mainly because it's simple, inexpensive, controls risk, and is pretty easy to understand.

Index Options can run for as long as 10 years. They provide diversity for a trader who can't or doesn't want to buy a varied portfolio of stocks. They are pure cash plays though. There is no opportunity to actually buy the underlying assets.

If you're interested in trading in Index Options, you might also consider learning about technical analysis, since it would be incredibly difficult to conduct a fundamental analysis of business in a typical stock index such as the S&P 500. Technical analysis on the other hand tracks the movement of stocks (or an index) over time and looks for indicators to help predict price fluctuations. A less sophisticated approach would be to simply look at the current economy, consider the behavior of the index, and invest or bet based on that. The S&P

500, for instance, has been steadily rising the past decade (it has been volatile though). So you might figure that so long as current business and economic conditions continue, buying an index option on that index is a fairly safe bet. Of course you aren't the only trader to figure that out, so you'll likely be paying a price reflecting that investor opinion. It's a low risk, low reward approach that doesn't require a lot of effort. Of course, if the index ends up falling (which does happen sooner or later), you could lose your whole investment. Using technical analysis might help you figure this out, relying on an index to keep doing what it's doing is less dependable.

Mini Index Options

While Index Options are a low cost entry into options trading, Mini Index Options and even less expensive. These options hold one-tenth the amount of stocks the Index Options hold and cost a little more than one-tenth the price.

Right now you have two choices if you want to trade Mini Index Options. There is a NASDAQ-100 version and an S&P 500 version.

Long Call Options

Writing Long Call Options is a simple, beginner, approach to investment. It can make it possible for an undercapitalized investor to benefit from price rises in highly priced stocks.

Let's say you think a certain stock is poised for an upward movement over the next year. Unfortunately for you the stock's $300 per share price would require the commitment of $30,000 of your money to buy 100 shares. Since most experts (me included), recommend not putting any more than 3% of your total investment capital into any one investment. This means any investor having less than $1,000,000 should think twice about putting $30,000 into any one investment.

Instead, you could buy a Long Call contract for about 10% of that amount. This would be a little more than $3,000. So long as your investment capital is at $300,000, the risk of $3,000 is justifiable. Remember though, if you'd bought the stock and it stagnated, or experienced a price drop, you'd still have most or all of your investment (example, the stock price falls a dollar a share, you've lost $100). In the same situation with your Long Call option, you'd lose the entire $3,000 investment. Of course if the stock price goes up a dollar, you'd stand to make a much greater profit via the option than you would if you owned the stock outright. As with any leveraged investment, you risk higher profits and higher losses than you do if you own the underlying asset.

Generally, a Long Call Option contract is a good choice if you're pretty confident the asset is going to rise in value. Suppose you identify pent up demand in a particular industry. You feel that companies that supply key products for this industry are poised to do well. You do your research and find one particular company that is in very good shape to take advantage of such a situation. The company's "fundamentals" look good. (Fundamentals are share price versus historical share price, price to earnings ration [P/E], cash flow, return on assets.) You decide it's a good bullish investment. You can either buy the actual stock, or purchase a Long Call on the stock. If the stock price advances as anticipated, you'll make money either way. You'll enjoy a greater percentage profit though via the options investment, than you will from the stock investment. Of course if the stock doesn't advance, you can still sell of the stock for a small to moderate loss, while you'll be out all the money you spent on the options contract.

Vertical Spreads

This is an overall strategy that forms the basis of a couple of bullish strategies. Playing a vertical spread calls for buying the same number of options on the exactly the same asset, but with different strike prices.

Bull Call Spread

If you're anticipating a price rise in a stock you're following, then a Bull Call Spread strategy is a moderate risk, moderate return approach. To use this technique, you buy a call option or options at a specific strike price, and also sell the same number of calls of the same asset at a higher strike price with the same expiration date.

This provides the possibility of realizing an upside return, while limiting downside risk to just the costs of the options. You make money if the stock price rises as anticipated before the expiration date of the options contracts. Your gain is limited though, by the higher strike price. If the price of the stock declines, then the options expire with no loss to you except for the price you paid for the options.

Bear Call Spread

In a Bear Call Spread, you're buying two identical calls except for their different strike prices. This is an income producing spread, based on the income produced by the lower priced, or "short" call. The higher priced, or "long" call, serves to limit the upside risk of the investment.

In this strategy, you make your money at the beginning, and then look to retain as much as you can before either closing out the position or watching the calls expire. You experience the maximum gain if the stock price remains below the lower call option price. If the stock does rise, the higher priced call option limits your maximum potential loss.

This is an appropriate strategy if you anticipate a stock's decline or stagnation. It is not a good choice if you think the stock price is going to go up.

Horizontal Spreads

A horizontal spread (also known as a "Calendar Spread) involves buying and selling options with the same characteristics except for the expiration dates. The trader makes money off the sale of shorter-term options and uses the purchase of a longer-term option to protect the investment.

Horizontal spreads are used during times of stagnation in a market. In buying and selling these options, you need to be comfortable with your understanding of the particular market and its likelihood of gaining or declining. There are two types of horizontal spreads.

Horizontal Call Spread

There are a couple of different approaches to a horizontal call spread. In one, you buy and sell options of different expiration dates and strike prices ("diagonal" call spread). In another, you buy and sell options of different expiration dates, but identical strike prices.

Let's say you've identified a stock that you think is going to hover around a specific price the next quarter or more. To execute a horizontal call spread, you would buy a call option for perhaps, three months out and sell a call option for one month away. You've realized some cash for the option you've sold, and put up some cash for the option you're purchased. At this point you've invested more than you've gained, since the longer option will cost more than the shorter one. So long as the stock stays stagnant though, you'll be able to sell the longer call for something less than the original price (as the expiration date nears, the value of the option declines).

Your risk is in stock price movement. If the underlying stock goes up or down a few dollars and stays at that price, then both options will end up expiring worthless. This means you're out your initial investment minus the money you received for the option you sold. You can't however, lose more than that amount (plus commissions of course).

Horizontal Put Spread

This is similar to the Horizontal Call Strategy, but you're buying a longer term put option and selling a shorter term put option. Also just like the other horizontal spread approach, you can adopt a diagonal or horizontal strategy.

Long Put Options

This is a strategy for when you think the market is headed into a sustained down turn (yes, it does happen). This is a very simple strategy and doesn't call for you to deal with margins or selling short and the issues that come with that method of investment.

The strategy is simple. Just buy a put option at the money for the stock whose price you believe is going to decline. If it does, you make money. If it doesn't, you're out the cost of the option. Compare this to shorting the same stock. You'll make a greater percentage gain if you're right, and be risking less money if you're wrong, plus you won't have to worry about a margin call or paying interest on your borrowed stock shares.

Iron Condor

Okay. It sounds like the title of a movie starring a couple of washed up action film stars, but it's really a viable options trading strategy for times when the market isn't moving in either direction.

To build your Iron Condor you need to set up a pair of credit spreads. The first is a call credit spread at an above the market price. The second is to sell a credit spread at a below the market price.

To create your first credit spread for the Iron Condor, buy an out of the money call and sell an out of the money call with an even higher strike price than the first call. To create your second, sell an out of the money put and buy an out of the money put with an even lower strike price than the first put. While I've used the terms "first" and "second," it isn't necessary to create the credit spreads in any particular order.

Your gain comes from the money you receive from selling the call and put of each spread. If the underlying stock's price remains between the strike prices of the shorter call and put, the options expire worthless and you maximize your profit.

Using Technical Indicators

Many options traders rely on technical indicators to help identify opportunities. Since options traders are particularly concerned with time because their options contracts only run for a specific period of time, they tend to concentrate on indicators that help them get a sense of which way securities are moving and how much momentum they have.

As an option trader, one of the most important things you can do is learn to identify over and under bought markets or stocks. One such approach is by using the Relative Strength Index or RSI.

Using the Relative Strength Index

This approach looks at just how big recent gains and losses for a particular stock have been. Traders who use an RSI approach favor stock options rather than index options. This is because it is easier to figure out whether a particular stock is over or under bought than it is an entire stock index, which usually contains dozens or hundreds of stocks.

You calculate RSI by starting with a value of 100. You then calculate the number of days where the stock closes up and divide that number by the number of days the stock closes down. Divide 100 by the result and that will give you a value between 0 and 100. When a stock moves above 30 on the scale, the trader assumes the stock is under bought and views it as a bullish signal. When a stock drops below 70, it's an over bought signal and the trader views it as a bearish signal.

A couple of things you should consider. For one, there's nothing that says you have to use 30 and 70 as your trigger points. More cautious investors might go with 20 and 80 to be even more confident. They may miss some opportunities with these triggers, but may also avoid some losses. Also, another thing many traders do, is look for some kind of confirmation signal, so they're not just relying on their trigger points.

There are technical analysis tools traders rely on to monitor stock momentum. One of these is a Candlestick Chart analysis. Candlesticks are symbols that show the trader the stock's opening price for the day, closing price for the day. This is shown via a rectangular box (candlestick) whose height is based on those prices. At each end of the candlestick are "wicks." These are vertically oriented lines that indicate the stock's high and low for the day. The candlestick also displays a color to indicate whether the stock price has risen or declined. Some systems use green and red, others use white and black. You can go to www.stockcharts.com to find a candlestick chart for a particular stock.

Candlesticks are useful for visualizing a stock's trend and investors mood about that stock. Traders look for different patterns created by the candlesticks over time. For instance, a pattern with three straight rising candlesticks, followed by a short rising candlestick and then a long declining candlestick that engulfs the range of the previous candlestick. Such a pattern is considered a bearish sign. If your RSI analysis indicates a sell point and you find a confirmation in a candlestick pattern, you can be a bit more confident about exiting your position.

You can also have a bullish candlestick pattern, which displays as the inverse of the bearish pattern. Candlestick analysis is an in-depth and useful approach to trend analysis. There are others though that are just as popular. This is really fodder for an intermediate level e-book.

It's time to wrap things up. In the last chapter you'll learn about common mistakes to avoid as an options trader.

Chapter 6:
Mistakes to Avoid

"The four most dangerous words in investing are: 'this time it's different.'" – Sir John Templeton

Every beginner makes mistakes. For beginning athletes, the risk is injury or embarrassment. For beginning musicians it might be banishment to the basement or the garage, while beginning chess players might face the ignominy of the "Fool's Mate."

That all pales to the consequences of beginner mistakes for an options trader. Your mistakes cost money. Your goal is to avoid as many of them as you can.

Failure to Have a Plan

At the very top of the list of beginner mistakes is playing on hunches or relying on instinct. Under the best of circumstances, an educated trader who does his or her homework is applying skill and knowledge to earn a profit investing in a market. At the worst, it's just gambling. You want to avoid gambling with your investment stake.

Learn about different approaches to trading. Study the market you think offers you the best opportunities and also study the assets that market holds. Create a trading plan for each investment you execute and make sure you have both an entry and an exit point set for that security.

Letting Emotion Rule Your Trades

Traders are human beings. It isn't surprising when one makes a decision based on emotion rather than brains. This is fine when you're picking lunch, but not when you're investing. If your gut tells you to get out of a position and your analysis tells you a turning point isn't far away, exit. If you gut says go and your analysis says "stay," ask yourself how much you trust your research and your understanding of the investment and base your decision on that.

The last two instances are times when maybe your gut is in the right ballpark. It's when it isn't, that traders get in trouble. Staying in a position because it's continuing a trend you saw, even though your analysis says the trend is ending, is letting an emotion (greed) override your reason. It seldom ends well. Jumping into an investment simply because you've been out of the market a few day and feel you're missing the action is another bad idea. You've learned about trading approaches for bull markets, bear markets, and stagnant markets in this e-book. If you can't find a good investment, stay out until you do.

Letting Fear or Greed Determine Your Trading Investment

Invest too little and you'll have trouble benefiting from your research and analysis. Invest too much and a loss could cripple you. This is one of the reasons many traders limit an individual trade to about 3% of their investment capital. This doesn't mean you have to follow that 3% example, but it does mean you need to take a cold hard look at your wallet and figure out what a reasonable amount of money to risk per trade is. If you can't, then by all means, use 3%.

Focusing Too Much on the Expiration Date

Knowing your option contract's expiration date is important of course. But failing to re-evaluate the conditions can be a mistake. If the reasons for your investment change, take another look. Is it still a good investment? Unexpected announcements and incidents can turn a situation upside down.

"Doubling Up" to Make Up Losses

Gamblers often double up on their bets in order to cover their losses. While this may be a workable strategy, if you have a big enough wallet and manage to have some good luck, it's not investing. As part of your trading plan, you've determined what percentage of your investment money you're willing to invest per trade. If you follow this plan, you'll increase you investments as your portfolio grows and decrease them if your portfolio declines. Both of these things are reasonable adjustments.

Conclusion

Thank you again for purchasing this book!

I hope this book was able to help you to start options trading successfully.

The next steps are to make your investment plan, find a broker, and start looking for your investment opportunity.

Finally, if you enjoyed this book, please take the time to share your thoughts and post a review on Amazon. It'd be greatly appreciated!

Thank you and good luck!

CPSIA information can be obtained
at www.ICGtesting.com
Printed in the USA
LVHW081210200920
666570LV00021B/3393

9 781537 578101